How To Stop Gambling

How To Stop Gambling
Copyright © Chris Allton, 2023
First published by Chris Allton 2023 via Amazon Kindle Direct Publishing
www.chrisallton.com
ISBN - 9798379157050

Front cover design © 2023 by Chris Allton

Contents

18. Forgive yourself

19. Stay focused on your goals

20. Never give up

Admit that you have a problem:

The first step in stopping gambling is acknowledging that you have a problem.

Gambling can be a fun and entertaining activity for many people. It provides a rush of excitement and the potential to win big, which can be very enticing. However, for some individuals, gambling can quickly turn into a destructive habit that can lead to financial ruin, strained relationships, and even addiction.

If you suspect that your gambling is becoming a problem, the first step towards recovery is admitting that you have a problem. This can be a difficult and humbling experience, but it is a necessary step in the journey towards regaining control of your life.

The following is a guide on how to admit that you have a gambling problem and take the first step towards recovery.

Recognize the signs of a gambling problem

Before you can admit that you have a problem, you must first recognize the signs of a gambling problem. Some of the most common signs include:

- Spending more time and money gambling than you originally intended
- Lying to loved ones about the amount of time and money spent gambling
- Feeling guilty or ashamed about your gambling behaviour
- Using gambling as a way to escape from problems or negative emotions

- Neglecting responsibilities and commitments in order to gamble
- Trying unsuccessfully to cut back or stop gambling altogether

If you identify with any of these signs, it may be time to admit that you have a gambling problem.

Understand the consequences of a gambling problem

Admitting that you have a problem with gambling can be a difficult and emotional process. It is important to understand that this admission is not a sign of weakness, but rather a step towards taking control of your life and addressing the consequences of your gambling behaviour.

A gambling problem can have serious consequences, both financially and emotionally. It can strain relationships with loved ones, cause financial hardship, and lead to feelings of depression and anxiety. By admitting that you have a problem, you are taking the first step towards addressing these consequences and preventing further damage.

Talk to a trusted friend or family member

Admitting that you have a gambling problem can be a scary and overwhelming experience. It may be helpful to talk to a trusted friend or family member about your struggles. This person can provide emotional support and encouragement as you begin the process of recovery.

It is important to choose someone who will be supportive and non-judgmental. This can be a difficult conversation to have, so it may be helpful to plan out what you want to say ahead of time.

Seek professional help

In addition to talking to a friend or family member, it may be helpful to seek professional help. There are many resources available to help individuals with gambling problems, including counsellors and support groups.

A professional can provide guidance and support as you work towards overcoming your gambling addiction. They can also help you develop coping strategies and a plan for moving forward.

Join a support group

Support groups can be a valuable resource for individuals struggling with gambling addiction. These groups provide a safe and supportive environment where individuals can share their experiences and receive encouragement from others who are going through similar struggles.

There are many different support groups available, including Gamblers Anonymous and SMART Recovery. These groups can be found online or in-person and are typically free to join.

Create a plan for recovery

Admitting that you have a gambling problem is just the first step in the recovery process. In order to truly overcome your addiction, you will need to create a plan for recovery.

This plan should include specific steps and goals for overcoming your addiction. It may include things like seeking professional help, joining a support group, setting financial goals, and finding healthy ways to cope with stress and negative emotions.

It is important to remember that recovery is a journey, and it may take time to fully overcome your addiction.

Make a commitment to quit:

Once you have admitted that you have a problem, make a commitment to quit gambling.

Gambling addiction is a serious problem that affects millions of people worldwide. Whether you gamble online, at a casino, or on sports, the addiction can take over your life and lead to devastating consequences. The good news is that quitting gambling is possible, and making a commitment to quit is the first step towards a healthier, happier life.

In this book, we will explore the process of making a commitment to quit gambling and provide you with practical tips and strategies to help you achieve your goal. We will also discuss the challenges you may face during your journey and offer guidance on how to overcome them.

Admitting that you have a problem with gambling can be difficult, but it is an essential step towards recovery. It takes courage and strength to acknowledge that you have lost control over your gambling habits and need help. Once you have taken this important step, the next step is to make a commitment to quit.

Making a commitment to quit gambling means setting a goal to stop gambling and taking active steps to achieve it. It involves making a firm decision and sticking to it, no matter how challenging it may be. Here are some tips to help you make a commitment to quit gambling:

1. Set a specific goal: It's essential to have a clear, specific goal in mind when you decide to quit gambling. Write down your goal and be as specific as possible. For example, you might set a goal to stop gambling for six months or to save a certain amount of money each week by not gambling.

2. Identify your triggers: Gambling addiction often has triggers that lead to the urge to gamble. Identifying these triggers is an important step in making a commitment to quit. Common triggers include stress, boredom, loneliness, or financial problems.

3. Seek support: It's crucial to have a support system when you decide to quit gambling. Reach out to friends or family

members who understand your struggle and can offer encouragement and support. Consider joining a support group or seeking the help of a professional counsellor.

4. Create a plan: A well-thought-out plan can help you stay on track and avoid relapse. Identify strategies that will help you cope with triggers and avoid temptation. Plan activities that you enjoy that don't involve gambling.

5. Stay motivated: Making a commitment to quit gambling is a long-term goal, and it's important to stay motivated. Celebrate your successes and remind yourself of the benefits of quitting. Visualize yourself free of the negative

consequences of gambling, such as debt, stress, and damaged relationships.

6. Take it one day at a time: Recovery from gambling addiction is a process that takes time. Focus on taking it one day at a time and celebrate small victories along the way.

Making a commitment to quit gambling is just the first step on a journey towards recovery. It's essential to be patient and kind to yourself during this process. You may experience setbacks or relapses, but it's important to remember that recovery is possible with determination and support.

In conclusion, quitting gambling is not easy, but it is possible. Making a commitment to quit is the first step towards a healthier, happier life. It involves setting a specific goal, identifying your triggers, seeking support, creating a plan, staying motivated, and taking it one day at a time. With the right mindset and support system, you can overcome your gambling addiction and achieve a life free of its negative consequences.

Identify your triggers:

Identify the triggers that lead you to gamble and avoid them as much as possible.

Gambling can be a fun and exciting activity for some, but for others, it can quickly turn into an addiction. If you find yourself unable to resist the urge to gamble, it's essential to take steps to break the cycle and regain control of your life. One of the most important steps you can take is to identify your triggers.

Triggers are the thoughts, feelings, situations, or people that can cause you to feel the urge to gamble. By learning to recognize these triggers, you can take steps to avoid or manage them and reduce the likelihood of relapse.

Here are some common triggers to watch out for:

1. Negative Emotions: Many people turn to gambling as a way to escape negative emotions such as stress, anxiety, or depression. When you feel overwhelmed by negative emotions, it's important to find healthy ways to cope, such as exercise, meditation, or talking to a friend.

2. Boredom: Gambling can also be a way to pass the time when you're bored. Instead of turning to gambling, try finding new hobbies or activities that you enjoy.

3. Social Pressure: Peer pressure can also be a trigger for gambling. If you have friends or family members who enjoy

gambling, it can be challenging to resist the urge to join in. Try to find new social activities that don't involve gambling or be honest with your loved ones about your struggles with addiction.

4. Financial Stress: If you're struggling with financial stress, gambling may seem like a way to solve your problems quickly. However, gambling is rarely a sustainable solution, and can often lead to further financial problems. Instead, seek help from a financial counsellor or therapist to develop a plan for managing your finances.

5. Excitement: The thrill of winning can be a powerful trigger for gambling addiction. However, the excitement of gambling is often short-lived, and can

quickly turn into disappointment and regret. Instead, seek out activities that provide a more sustained sense of accomplishment, such as exercise or creative pursuits.

Once you've identified your triggers, it's important to take steps to avoid or manage them. Here are some strategies you can try:

1. Avoid Triggers: If possible, try to avoid situations or people that trigger your urge to gamble. For example, if you know that a particular casino or gambling website is a trigger, stay away from it. Or, if you have friends who encourage you to gamble, try to limit your time with them.

2. Develop Coping Skills: Instead of turning to gambling to cope with negative

emotions or stress, develop healthy coping skills such as exercise, meditation, or talking to a friend. Practice these skills regularly so that they become second nature.

3. Create a Support Network: Having a support network of friends and family members who understand your struggles with gambling can be incredibly helpful. Joining a support group or seeking therapy can also be beneficial.

4. Stay Busy: When you're busy with other activities, you're less likely to feel the urge to gamble. Find new hobbies or activities that you enjoy and make them a regular part of your routine.

5. Make a Plan: Develop a plan for managing your triggers and preventing

relapse. Write down your plan and refer to it regularly as a reminder of your goals and strategies.

Remember, breaking the cycle of gambling addiction is a process, and it may take time and effort to make lasting changes. However, by identifying your triggers and taking steps to avoid or manage them, you can take control of your life and overcome your addiction.

Create a support network:

Surround yourself with people who support your decision to quit gambling.

Gambling addiction is a serious issue that affects millions of people around the world. It is a condition that can destroy lives, relationships, and finances. While many individuals try to quit gambling on their own, the road to recovery is often long and challenging. One of the most effective ways to overcome a gambling addiction is to create a support network.

A support network is a group of people who are committed to helping you quit gambling and achieve your recovery goals. This can include friends, family members, counsellors, support group members, and other individuals who have experience with gambling addiction. The following are some tips on how to create a strong and effective support network.

1. Be honest with your loved ones One of the first steps in creating a support network is to be honest with your loved ones about your gambling addiction. Let them know that you are committed to quitting and that you need their support. Being open and honest about your struggles can help you build trust and strengthen your relationships.

2. Seek professional help In addition to relying on the support of friends and family members, it is essential to seek professional help. A counsellor or therapist can help you develop coping

skills and strategies to deal with cravings and triggers. They can also provide you with valuable insight and guidance as you work towards recovery.

3. Attend support group meetings Support group meetings can be a valuable resource for individuals struggling with gambling addiction. These meetings provide a safe and supportive environment where you can share your experiences, learn from others, and receive encouragement and support. Consider attending Gamblers Anonymous or other similar groups to connect with others who are facing similar challenges.

4. Find positive role models Another effective way to create a support network

is to find positive role models. This can include individuals who have successfully overcome a gambling addiction or those who have never struggled with gambling. Surrounding yourself with positive influences can help you stay motivated and focused on your recovery goals.

5. Avoid negative influences While it is important to find positive role models, it is equally important to avoid negative influences. This can include individuals who still gamble, those who are unsupportive of your recovery efforts, or those who are negative and pessimistic. Surround yourself with individuals who uplift and encourage you rather than drag you down.

6. Communicate regularly with your support network Regular communication is essential to building a strong and effective support network. Make sure to keep in touch with your loved ones, attend support group meetings, and stay in contact with your therapist or counsellor. Let your support network know when you are struggling or feeling tempted to gamble so that they can provide you with the help and encouragement you need.

7. Celebrate your successes Finally, it is important to celebrate your successes along the way. Every step towards recovery is a significant accomplishment, and you should be proud of yourself for taking the necessary steps to overcome

your gambling addiction. Share your victories with your support network and celebrate together.

In conclusion, creating a strong and effective support network is essential to overcoming a gambling addiction. It is a process that requires honesty, vulnerability, and commitment. By seeking professional help, attending support group meetings, finding positive role models, avoiding negative influences, communicating regularly, and celebrating your successes, you can build a support network that will help you achieve your recovery goals and lead a fulfilling life. Remember, you are not alone in your journey towards recovery, and with the right support, you can overcome your gambling addiction and build a brighter future.

Seek professional help:

Consider seeking professional help from a therapist or counsellor who specializes in treating gambling addiction.

Gambling addiction is a serious problem that affects millions of people around the world. The addiction can be devastating, causing financial problems, relationship issues, and even leading to mental health problems such as anxiety and depression. If you or someone you know is struggling with a gambling addiction, seeking professional help is crucial. A therapist or counsellor who specializes in treating gambling addiction can provide support and guidance to help you overcome this addiction and regain control of your life.

When seeking professional help for gambling addiction, it is important to choose a therapist or counsellor who is experienced in treating this specific addiction. Many therapists and counsellors may have experience with addiction treatment, but gambling addiction is a unique problem that requires specialized treatment. Look for a therapist who has specific training or experience in treating gambling addiction.

One of the benefits of seeking professional help for gambling addiction is that you will have access to a trained professional who can provide guidance and support throughout the recovery process. A therapist or counsellor can help you identify the root causes of your addiction, develop coping strategies to manage triggers and urges to gamble, and work with you to develop a plan for achieving and maintaining long-term recovery.

In addition to individual therapy, group therapy can also be a helpful component of gambling addiction treatment. Many therapists and counsellors offer support groups for individuals struggling with gambling addiction. These groups provide a safe and supportive environment where individuals can share their experiences, receive encouragement and support, and learn from others who are going through similar struggles.

Cognitive-behavioural therapy (CBT) is a commonly used approach in the treatment of gambling addiction. CBT focuses on changing patterns of thinking and behaviour that contribute to the addiction. By identifying negative thought patterns and replacing them with more positive, adaptive thoughts, individuals can learn to manage triggers and urges to gamble.

Another effective approach to gambling addiction treatment is motivational interviewing. This technique is focused on helping individuals identify their own reasons for wanting to change and supporting them in developing the motivation to make changes in their behaviour. By focusing on the individual's personal values and goals, motivational interviewing can help individuals stay committed to their recovery.

In some cases, medication may also be used as part of the treatment plan for gambling addiction. Certain medications, such as antidepressants, have been found to be effective in reducing the symptoms of gambling addiction. However, medication should always be used in conjunction with therapy and under the guidance of a trained healthcare provider.

While seeking professional help for gambling addiction can be a difficult step to take, it is an important one for anyone who wants to overcome this addiction and regain control of their life. With the help of a trained therapist or counsellor, individuals can develop the tools and strategies they need to manage their addiction and achieve lasting recovery.

Join a support group:

Join a support group for people with gambling addiction, such as Gamblers Anonymous.

Gambling addiction is a serious problem that can ruin lives and cause a lot of damage to relationships, finances, and mental health. If you or someone you know is struggling with gambling addiction, it's essential to get help and support as soon as possible. One of the most effective ways to overcome this problem is by joining a support group.

Support groups are communities of people who share similar experiences, challenges, and goals. They provide a safe and supportive environment where members can express their feelings, get advice, and connect with others who understand what they're going through. In the case of gambling addiction, support groups can be a lifeline for those who feel alone, ashamed, and overwhelmed by their problem.

Gamblers Anonymous (GA) is one of the most well-known and effective support groups for people with gambling addiction. Founded in 1957, GA has helped millions of people worldwide to overcome their addiction and rebuild their lives. The program is based on the 12-step approach, which is similar to the one used by Alcoholics Anonymous (AA).

The 12-step approach is a spiritual program that emphasizes personal responsibility, humility, and surrender to a higher power. It encourages members to take an honest and fearless inventory of their life, admit their wrongdoings, make amends, and seek forgiveness. The program also emphasizes the importance of connecting with other members and helping them on their journey of recovery.

Joining GA is easy and free. All you need to do is attend a meeting, which are held regularly in most cities and towns around the world. You can find a meeting near you by visiting the GA website or by contacting a local helpline. GA meetings are anonymous, confidential, and open to anyone who wants to stop gambling.

At GA meetings, you'll find a diverse group of people who share your struggles and your goals. You'll be welcomed warmly and treated with respect and understanding. The meetings are led by volunteer members who have been through the program themselves and are committed to helping others. They'll share their stories, offer advice, and provide support and encouragement.

In addition to attending meetings, GA members are encouraged to follow the program's principles in their daily lives. This includes avoiding triggers, such as gambling establishments or online gambling sites, and seeking help when needed. The program also recommends making positive changes in your life, such as improving your relationships, finding new hobbies, and taking care of your physical and mental health.

One of the most significant benefits of joining GA is the sense of community and belonging that it provides. Addiction can be a lonely and isolating experience, but being part of a support group can make a big difference. You'll be surrounded by people who understand what you're going through and who are committed to helping you. You'll also have the opportunity to help others, which can be incredibly rewarding and fulfilling.

Another benefit of joining GA is the accountability that it provides. The program encourages members to take responsibility for their actions and to be accountable to others. This can be a powerful motivator to stay on track and to make positive changes in your life. It can also help you to avoid relapse and to maintain your sobriety over the long term.

In conclusion, if you're struggling with gambling addiction, joining a support group like Gamblers Anonymous can be a game-changer. It can provide the support, guidance, and community that you need to overcome your addiction and to rebuild your life. Remember, you're not alone, and there is help available. Take the first step today and attend a GA meeting. Your future self will thank you.

Set realistic goals:

Set realistic goals for yourself, such as going a certain amount of time without gambling.

Gambling addiction is a serious problem that can cause significant financial and emotional distress.

For individuals who are struggling with this addiction, setting realistic goals is an essential step towards recovery.

When setting goals for yourself, it is important to ensure that they are achievable and measurable. Here are some tips for setting realistic goals to help you stop gambling.

1. Start with small goals

When setting goals, it can be tempting to aim for the stars. However, if you are just beginning your journey towards recovery, it is important to start with small goals that you can achieve. For example, you could set a goal to go a day or a week without gambling. Once you have achieved this goal, you can gradually increase the length of time that you go without gambling.

2. Make your goals specific and measurable

When setting goals, it is important to make them specific and measurable. For example, instead of setting a goal to "stop gambling," you could set a goal to "go two weeks without visiting a casino." This goal is specific and measurable, which makes it easier to track your progress.

3. Write down your goals

Writing down your goals is a great way to make them more concrete. When you write down your goals, you are making a commitment to yourself to achieve them. You can also refer back to your written goals when you need motivation or a reminder of why you are trying to stop gambling.

4. Set deadlines for your goals

Setting deadlines for your goals can help you stay on track and motivated. For example, you could set a goal to go a month without gambling and give yourself a deadline to achieve this goal. Having a deadline can also help you break down your goal into smaller, more manageable steps.

5. Celebrate your successes

When you achieve a goal, it is important to celebrate your success. Celebrating your successes can help you stay motivated and focused on your goals. For example, you could reward yourself with a small treat or activity when you achieve a goal.

6. Be prepared for setbacks

Setbacks are a natural part of the recovery process. It is important to be prepared for setbacks and to have a plan in place for how you will handle them. For example, if you experience a setback, you could reach out to a support group or a therapist for help.

7. Keep track of your progress

Keeping track of your progress is an important part of setting and achieving goals. You could keep a journal or use a tracking app to record your progress. Seeing how far you have come can help you stay motivated and focused on your goals.

8. Seek support

Seeking support from friends, family members, or a therapist can be helpful when you are setting and achieving goals. Support can help you stay accountable and provide encouragement when you need it. You can also join a support group for individuals who are struggling with gambling addiction.

9. Stay committed to your goals

Staying committed to your goals can be challenging, but it is essential for long-term success. Remind yourself why you are trying to stop gambling and stay focused on your goals. When you feel tempted to gamble, remind yourself of the progress you have made and the goals you are working towards.

10. Be patient with yourself

Recovery is a process, and it takes time. It is important to be patient with yourself and to acknowledge that there will be ups and downs along the way. Remember that setting and achieving goals is a journey, and it is okay to take things one step at a time.

In conclusion, setting realistic goals is an important step towards recovery from gambling addiction. When setting goals, it is important to start with small, achievable goals and to make them specific and measurable.

Develop healthy habits:

Develop healthy habits to replace your gambling behaviour, such as exercise, reading, or spending time with friends and family.

Gambling can be a dangerous addiction that affects not only the individual, but also their loved ones. It can lead to financial ruin, emotional distress, and social isolation. Fortunately, there are steps you can take to overcome your gambling addiction and develop healthy habits to replace this destructive behaviour.

Developing healthy habits is a vital component of recovering from any addiction, including gambling. It helps to create a sense of structure and routine in your daily life, which can help you stay focused and motivated on your journey to recovery. Here are some healthy habits that you can incorporate into your life to help you stop gambling:

1. Exercise regularly Exercise is a great way to relieve stress and reduce anxiety, which can be powerful triggers for gambling. It also releases endorphins, which can improve your mood and increase your sense of well-being. Find an exercise that you enjoy and make it a regular part of your routine. Whether it's going for a run, taking a yoga class, or lifting weights, exercise can help you stay on track and feel better both physically and mentally.

2. Read books Reading is a great way to occupy your mind and focus on something positive. Choose books that interest you and that can help you learn new skills or improve your knowledge in a particular area. Reading can also help you relax and reduce stress, which can be especially helpful during moments of temptation to gamble.

3. Spend time with friends and family One of the biggest challenges of gambling addiction is the social isolation that can come with it. To combat this, make an effort to spend time with friends and family on a regular basis. Surrounding yourself with supportive people who care about you can be incredibly beneficial for your mental and emotional

well-being. It can also help you stay accountable and motivated to stay on track with your recovery.

4. Find new hobbies Gambling can take up a lot of time and energy, so finding new hobbies can be a great way to fill that void. Choose something that interests you and that you can do regularly. This could be anything from painting to playing a musical instrument to learning a new language. The key is to find something that you enjoy and that can help you focus on something positive.

5. Seek professional help Finally, don't hesitate to seek professional help if you feel that you need it. Gambling addiction can be a complex and challenging issue, and it may require the support of a

trained professional to help you overcome it. Consider seeing a therapist or joining a support group to help you stay motivated and on track with your recovery.

In conclusion, developing healthy habits is an essential component of overcoming gambling addiction. Exercise, reading, spending time with friends and family, finding new hobbies, and seeking professional help are all effective ways to replace your gambling behaviour with positive habits. Remember that recovery is a journey, and it may take time and effort to get there. But with the right tools and support, you can overcome your addiction and lead a healthier, happier life.

Stay busy:

Stay busy to avoid thoughts of gambling.

Gambling addiction is a serious issue that affects millions of people worldwide. While there are many treatment options available, staying busy and occupied can be a powerful tool in helping individuals overcome their addiction. In this chapter, we will explore different ways to stay busy and avoid thoughts of gambling.

1. Find a new hobby: One of the best ways to stay busy is to find a new hobby. Engaging in activities that you enjoy and are passionate about can help take your mind off gambling. Whether it's painting, playing sports, or gardening, find an

activity that you enjoy and dedicate time to it.

2. Volunteer: Volunteering is another great way to stay busy and make a positive impact on your community. Find an organization that aligns with your interests and dedicate some of your time to helping them out. Not only will this give you a sense of purpose, but it will also help you meet new people and form new relationships.

3. Exercise: Regular exercise not only helps improve your physical health but also your mental health. Exercise releases endorphins, which can help reduce stress and anxiety. Find a workout routine that you enjoy and stick to it. Whether it's going for a run, hitting the gym, or taking

a yoga class, find a way to incorporate exercise into your daily routine.

4. Learn a new skill: Learning a new skill can be both challenging and rewarding. Take up a new language, learn to play an instrument, or enrol in a cooking class. The possibilities are endless. Not only will this help keep your mind occupied, but it will also give you a sense of accomplishment and boost your self-esteem.

5. Spend time with loved ones: Spending time with loved ones can be a great way to stay busy and distracted from gambling thoughts. Plan outings with friends and family, have a game night, or simply have a movie marathon. Being around people who care about you and

support you can help lift your spirits and keep you on track.

6. Start a journal: Journaling can be a powerful tool in overcoming addiction. Writing down your thoughts and feelings can help you process emotions and gain perspective. It can also serve as a reminder of your progress and how far you have come. Set aside time each day to write in your journal and reflect on your journey.

7. Practice mindfulness: Mindfulness is the practice of being present and fully engaged in the moment. It can help reduce stress and anxiety and increase feelings of happiness and contentment. Find a mindfulness practice that works for you, whether it's meditation, yoga, or

simply taking a few deep breaths. Incorporate mindfulness into your daily routine to help stay grounded and focused.

8. Read: Reading can be a great way to escape and take your mind off gambling. Whether it's a novel, a self-help book, or a biography, find something that interests you and dive in. Reading can help expand your knowledge, improve your vocabulary, and even reduce stress.

9. Set goals: Setting goals can help give you a sense of purpose and direction. Whether it's a long-term goal or a short-term goal, setting goals can help motivate you and give you something to work towards. Make sure your goals are

realistic and achievable and celebrate your progress along the way.

10. Seek support: Finally, it's important to seek support from others as you work to overcome your gambling addiction. Whether it's a therapist, a support group, or a trusted friend or family member, having someone to talk to and lean on can be a valuable resource. Don't be afraid to reach out for help when you need it.

Learn to manage your emotions:

Learn to manage your emotions in healthy ways, such as meditation, journaling, or talking to a friend.

Gambling addiction can be a serious problem for many individuals. It can cause financial ruin, strain relationships, and even lead to legal trouble. However, the underlying causes of gambling addiction often go deeper than just a love of the game or a desire for quick money. Emotions can play a significant role in fuelling a gambling addiction, and learning how to manage these emotions in healthy ways is key to overcoming the addiction.

One of the most important steps to managing emotions is learning to recognize them. Many gamblers use gambling as a way to avoid dealing with their emotions, and this can create a vicious cycle that only reinforces the addiction. By learning to recognize and acknowledge emotions, individuals can begin to take control of their behaviour and make healthier choices.

Meditation is one effective way to manage emotions. Meditation is a practice that involves focusing the mind and calming the body. By practicing meditation regularly, individuals can learn to quiet their racing thoughts and become more present in the moment. This can be particularly helpful for gamblers who may be prone to impulsive behaviour.

Journaling is another effective way to manage emotions. Writing down thoughts and feelings can help individuals gain a deeper understanding of themselves and their behaviour. Journaling can also be a helpful tool for tracking progress and identifying patterns in behaviour. For gamblers, keeping a journal can help them identify triggers that lead to gambling and develop strategies for avoiding those triggers in the future.

Talking to a friend or therapist can also be an effective way to manage emotions. Sharing feelings with someone who is supportive and non-judgmental can be a powerful way to release emotions and gain perspective. A therapist can also provide tools and techniques for managing emotions and developing healthy coping mechanisms.

In addition to these techniques, it's important to develop a strong support system. Many gamblers feel isolated and alone, and having a group of friends or family members who are supportive can be invaluable. Joining a support group for gambling addiction can also provide a sense of community and accountability.

Managing emotions is a lifelong process, and there will be times when even the most well-prepared individuals struggle. During these times, it's important to have a plan in place for managing the urge to gamble. This might involve distracting oneself with a different activity, reaching out to a friend, or simply taking a deep breath and reminding oneself of the reasons why quitting gambling is important.

Ultimately, learning to manage emotions is key to overcoming gambling addiction. By developing healthy coping mechanisms and a strong support system, individuals can take control of their behaviour and create a more fulfilling and satisfying life. If you or someone you know is struggling with gambling addiction, reach out for help today.

Avoid gambling environments:

Avoid places where gambling is present, such as casinos or online gambling websites.

Gambling can be a serious addiction that can cause significant problems in someone's life. Whether it is a habit or a full-blown addiction, gambling can lead to financial, emotional, and psychological issues that can be difficult to overcome. One of the best ways to stop gambling is to avoid the environments where it is present.

The first and most obvious environment to avoid is casinos. These establishments are designed to be tempting and attractive to gamblers, with flashy lights, music, and constant activity. The environment can be overwhelming and can trigger the urge to gamble. Even if you go to a casino with the intention of not gambling, the atmosphere and temptation can be too much to resist. It's best to stay away from casinos altogether if you're trying to stop gambling.

Another environment to avoid is online gambling websites. The internet has made gambling more accessible than ever before, with hundreds of websites offering various types of games and sports betting options. Online gambling can be especially dangerous because it is available 24/7, and you can gamble from the comfort of your own home. It's important to avoid online gambling websites and to block them from your computer and smartphone to reduce the temptation to gamble.

Other places to avoid include bars and pubs that have slot machines and video poker machines. These machines can be just as addictive as casino games and can lead to the same problems. If you're trying to stop gambling, it's best to avoid these establishments altogether or to go with friends who can help you stay accountable.

It's also important to avoid environments where gambling is normalized or celebrated. For example, if you have friends who are avid gamblers or who talk about gambling frequently, it can be difficult to resist the urge to join in. It's best to distance yourself from these types of people and to find new hobbies and interests that don't involve gambling.

One environment that can be difficult to avoid is the workplace. Many workplaces have office pools, lottery ticket purchases, or even on-site casinos. If you work in an environment where gambling is prevalent, it's important to set clear boundaries for yourself and to communicate your intentions to your co-workers. You may need to avoid certain social events or make it clear that you're not interested in participating in gambling activities.

Finally, it's important to avoid situations that may trigger the urge to gamble. For example, if you're going through a stressful time, you may be more likely to turn to gambling as a coping mechanism. It's important to recognize these triggers and to develop healthier coping mechanisms, such as exercise, meditation, or spending time with loved ones.

In conclusion, avoiding gambling environments is one of the most effective ways to stop gambling. This means staying away from casinos, online gambling websites, bars and pubs with gambling machines, and other environments where gambling is present. It's also important to distance yourself from people who normalize or celebrate gambling and to recognize and avoid situations that may trigger the urge to gamble. By taking these steps, you can reduce the temptation to gamble and take control of your life.

Cut off access to money:

Cut off access to money by closing credit cards, setting up a budget, or asking someone to hold your money for you.

Gambling addiction is a serious problem that can have devastating consequences. It can lead to financial ruin, relationship breakdowns, and even mental health issues. For those struggling with gambling addiction, cutting off access to money is an important step in breaking the cycle of addiction. In this chapter, we will explore some strategies for cutting off access to money and regaining control of your finances.

The first step in cutting off access to money is to close credit cards. Credit cards can be a temptation for those struggling with gambling addiction, as they provide access to credit that can be used to fund gambling activities. By closing credit cards, you remove this temptation and make it more difficult to access funds for gambling purposes.

To close a credit card, you will need to contact the issuer and request that the account be closed. Be aware that closing a credit card can impact your credit score, so it is important to consider this before taking this step. However, the long-term benefits of breaking the cycle of addiction far outweigh any short-term impacts on your credit score.

Another strategy for cutting off access to money is to set up a budget. A budget is a plan for how you will allocate your income and expenses. By creating a budget, you can identify areas where you may be overspending and redirect those funds to other areas of your life.

To create a budget, start by listing your income sources and your expenses. This can include things like rent, utilities, food, transportation, and entertainment. Once you have a clear picture of your income and expenses, you can begin to identify areas where you can cut back.

For example, if you are spending a significant amount of money on entertainment, you may be able to reduce this expense by finding free or low-cost activities to do instead. By redirecting these funds to other areas of your life, you can reduce the amount of money available for gambling activities.

Finally, another strategy for cutting off access to money is to ask someone to hold your money for you. This can be a friend, family member, or even a professional such as a financial advisor. By entrusting your funds to someone else, you remove the temptation to use them for gambling purposes.

Before entrusting your funds to someone else, be sure to choose someone you trust and who understands the seriousness of your addiction. You may also want to consider setting up a legal agreement to ensure that your funds are being held securely and used for the purposes you intend.

In conclusion, cutting off access to money is a critical step in breaking the cycle of addiction and regaining control of your finances. By closing credit cards, setting up a budget, or entrusting your funds to someone else, you can reduce the temptation to use your funds for gambling activities and redirect your resources to other areas of your life. Remember, breaking the cycle of addiction takes time and effort, but with the right strategies and support, it is possible to overcome gambling addiction and live a healthier, happier life.

Identify the consequences of gambling:

Identify the consequences of gambling, such as financial problems, relationship issues, or legal troubles.

Gambling is a thrilling activity that can easily turn into a destructive habit. For some people, it starts as harmless entertainment, but it can quickly spiral out of control and lead to significant problems. The consequences of gambling are numerous and can affect every aspect of a person's life, including their financial stability, relationships, and legal standing. In this book, we will explore the various consequences of gambling and offer advice on how to identify and address them.

Financial Problems:

One of the most immediate and apparent consequences of gambling is the financial strain it can cause. Gambling can quickly become an expensive habit, and it's not uncommon for people to spend more than they can afford on this activity. Those who gamble regularly may find themselves using credit cards, taking out loans, or borrowing money from friends and family to cover their losses. This behaviour can quickly spiral out of control and lead to a significant amount of debt.

In order to identify financial problems related to gambling, it's essential to monitor your spending habits carefully. If you find yourself spending more than you can afford, using credit cards or loans to gamble, or regularly dipping into your savings to cover losses, then you may have a problem. Additionally, if you notice that your bills are piling up, you're unable to pay rent or mortgage payments, or you're struggling to keep up with basic expenses, it may be time to seek help.

Relationship Issues:

Gambling can also cause a strain on relationships. Those who gamble regularly may become distant from their loved ones, preoccupied with their next bet or win. Additionally, financial problems caused by gambling can lead to arguments, stress, and tension within the family.

If you're experiencing relationship issues related to gambling, it's important to recognize the problem and take action. This may involve seeking therapy or counselling to work through any underlying issues or conflicts. Additionally, it's crucial to communicate openly and honestly with your loved ones about your gambling habits, and to make an effort to spend quality time with them.

Legal Troubles:

Finally, gambling can also lead to legal troubles. This is particularly true for those who gamble illegally or in unregulated environments. Gambling-related offenses can include things like fraud, embezzlement, or money laundering. Additionally, those who gamble may find themselves in legal trouble if they're unable to pay debts or fines related to their gambling activities.

If you're concerned about legal issues related to gambling, it's essential to seek legal advice as soon as possible. This may involve contacting a lawyer who specializes in gambling-related offenses, or seeking advice from a legal aid organization.

In addition to these consequences, gambling can also lead to a range of mental health issues, including anxiety, depression, and addiction. It's essential to be aware of the risks associated with gambling and to take action if you believe that you or a loved one may be experiencing problems related to this activity.

In conclusion, gambling can be a fun and exciting activity, but it can quickly turn into a destructive habit. The consequences of gambling can be severe and can affect every aspect of a person's life, including their financial stability, relationships, and legal standing. By identifying the potential consequences of gambling and taking action to address them, individuals can avoid the negative effects of this activity and lead happy, healthy lives.

Practice self-care:

Practice self-care to reduce stress and improve your overall well-being.

Gambling addiction is a serious issue that affects many people around the world. Whether you're struggling with a mild gambling problem or a full-blown addiction, it's important to take steps to overcome it. One of the most effective ways to stop gambling is by practicing self-care.

Self-care is the act of taking care of yourself, both physically and mentally. It involves doing things that make you feel good, reduce stress, and improve your overall well-being. When you practice self-care, you're investing in your own health and happiness. Here are some tips for practicing self-care to help you stop gambling.

1. Exercise regularly

Exercise is one of the most effective ways to reduce stress and improve your mental health. When you exercise, your body releases endorphins, which are natural feel-good chemicals. This can help to reduce feelings of anxiety and depression, which are often associated with gambling addiction. Regular exercise can also help you to sleep better, which is important for your overall well-being.

2. Get enough sleep

Sleep is essential for your physical and mental health. When you don't get enough sleep, you're more likely to feel irritable, anxious, and stressed. This can make it harder to resist the urge to gamble. Aim to get at least 7-8 hours of sleep each night. If you have trouble sleeping, try to establish a bedtime routine that helps you to relax before bed.

3. Eat a healthy diet

Eating a healthy diet can help to improve your mood and reduce stress. When you eat a balanced diet that includes plenty of fruits, vegetables, and whole grains, you're giving your body the nutrients it needs to function properly.

This can help to reduce feelings of anxiety and depression, which can be triggers for gambling.

4. Practice mindfulness

Mindfulness is the act of being present in the moment and focusing on your thoughts and feelings. When you practice mindfulness, you're able to observe your thoughts without judgment. This can be helpful when you're trying to overcome a gambling addiction, as it can help you to recognize your triggers and make better decisions.

5. Connect with others

Social support is important for your mental health. When you're going through a difficult time, it's important to have people you can talk to and rely on. This can help to reduce feelings of isolation and loneliness, which can be triggers for gambling. Try to connect with others who share your interests or hobbies or join a support group for people who are struggling with a gambling addiction.

6. Find healthy ways to cope with stress

Stress is a normal part of life, but when you're dealing with a gambling addiction, it can be overwhelming. Finding healthy ways to cope with stress can help you to avoid turning to gambling as a way to escape. Some healthy ways to cope with stress include exercise, meditation, deep breathing, or engaging in a hobby you enjoy.

7. Set goals for yourself

Setting goals for yourself can help you to stay focused on your recovery. It can also help you to feel a sense of accomplishment and pride when you achieve your goals. Start by setting small, achievable goals, such as going for a walk every day or avoiding gambling for a certain amount of time. As you achieve these goals, you can set bigger ones that will help you to reach your ultimate goal of overcoming your gambling addiction.

In conclusion, practicing self-care is an essential part of overcoming a gambling addiction. By taking care of your physical and mental health, you can reduce stress and improve your overall well-being. Remember that recovery is a journey, and it's important to be patient and kind to yourself as you work towards your goals. With the right support and a commitment to self-care, you can overcome your gambling addiction and live a healthy, fulfilling life.

Take responsibility for your actions:

Take responsibility for your actions and hold yourself accountable for your behaviour.

Responsibility is the act of acknowledging your actions and taking ownership of the consequences that come with them. It is the foundation of personal growth and is essential for living a fulfilling life. When it comes to gambling addiction, taking responsibility means acknowledging that you have a problem and that you need help. It also means recognizing the impact that your addiction has on others, such as family members, friends, and co-workers.

Why Taking Responsibility is Important

Taking responsibility is important for several reasons. First, it allows you to take control of your life and make positive changes. When you accept responsibility for your actions, you empower yourself to make better choices and to take steps to overcome your addiction. Second, taking responsibility shows others that you are committed to change. It can help rebuild trust and strengthen relationships. Finally, taking responsibility is essential for maintaining long-term recovery. By holding yourself accountable, you can stay focused on your goals and avoid falling back into old patterns of behaviour.

Tips for Taking Responsibility

1. Admit that you have a problem: The first step in taking responsibility is to admit that you have a problem with gambling. This can be difficult, but it is essential for moving forward.

2. Seek help: Once you have admitted that you have a problem, seek help from a professional or support group. There are many resources available for those struggling with gambling addiction, and reaching out for help is a sign of strength, not weakness.

3. Be honest with yourself and others: Honesty is crucial when it comes to taking responsibility. Be honest with yourself about your addiction and the impact it has on your life. Also, be honest

with others, such as family members and friends, about your struggles.

4. Set goals: Setting goals is an important part of taking responsibility. It gives you something to work towards and helps you stay focused on your recovery.

5. Take action: Taking action is the most crucial step in taking responsibility. Make a plan for how you will overcome your addiction, and then take action to make it happen.

Taking responsibility for your actions is essential for overcoming gambling addiction. It allows you to take control of your life, make positive changes, and maintain long-term recovery. By admitting that you have a problem, seeking help, being honest with yourself and others, setting goals, and taking action, you can overcome your addiction and live a fulfilling life. Remember that taking responsibility is a process, and it takes time and effort. But with persistence and dedication, you can take control of your life and overcome your addiction.

Learn from past mistakes:

Learn from past mistakes and use them as lessons to prevent future relapses.

Gambling addiction can be a serious problem for many people, and it can be difficult to overcome. It's easy to get caught up in the excitement and thrill of gambling, but the consequences of addiction can be devastating. For those who are struggling with gambling addiction, it's important to learn from past mistakes and use them as lessons to prevent future relapses.

The first step to overcoming gambling addiction is acknowledging that there is a problem. Many people who struggle with gambling addiction deny that they have a problem or believe that they can control their gambling. However, acknowledging that there is a problem is essential to recovery.

Once you have acknowledged that you have a problem with gambling, it's important to reflect on your past behaviour and identify the patterns that led to your addiction. Take some time to think about the situations or triggers that led you to gamble, such as stress, boredom, or social pressure.

Identifying these triggers can help you recognize them in the future and take steps to avoid them. For example, if stress is a trigger for your gambling, you may need to find healthier ways to cope with stress, such as exercise, meditation, or therapy.

It's also important to reflect on the consequences of your gambling addiction. Think about the impact it has had on your relationships, finances, and overall well-being. This reflection can be painful, but it's an essential part of the healing process.

After reflecting on your past behaviour, it's important to create a plan for the future. This plan should include strategies for avoiding triggers, coping with urges to gamble, and building a support network.

One effective strategy for avoiding triggers is to create a schedule or routine that fills your time with healthy activities. This can include exercise, hobbies, or spending time with friends and family.

Coping with urges to gamble can be challenging, but there are strategies that can help. One effective technique is to distract yourself with a different activity when you feel the urge to gamble. This could be something as simple as taking a walk, listening to music, or reading a book.

Building a support network is also essential to recovery. This can include friends, family, or a support group for those struggling with gambling addiction. Talking to others who understand what you're going through can be incredibly helpful.

It's important to remember that recovery is a process and it's normal to experience setbacks. If you do relapse, it's important to learn from the experience and use it as a lesson to prevent future relapses.

One effective way to learn from a relapse is to identify the triggers that led to the relapse and take steps to avoid them in the future. It's also important to reflect on the consequences of the relapse and use that as motivation to continue on the path to recovery.

Another important aspect of learning from past mistakes is to practice self-compassion. Be kind to yourself and remember that addiction is a disease that requires treatment and support. It's okay to make mistakes, as long as you learn from them and use them as lessons for the future.

In conclusion, gambling addiction can be a difficult problem to overcome, but it's possible with the right strategies and support. Learning from past mistakes and using them as lessons for the future is an essential part of the recovery process. Remember to acknowledge the problem, reflect on past behaviour, create a plan for the future, and practice self-compassion. With these tools, you can overcome gambling addiction and live a healthy, fulfilling life.

Celebrate your successes:

Celebrate your successes, no matter how small, to stay motivated.

Gambling addiction is a serious problem that affects millions of people around the world. For those who struggle with this addiction, the desire to gamble can be overwhelming, and the consequences can be devastating.

However, there are steps that you can take to overcome this addiction and take control of your life.

One of the most important of these steps is learning to celebrate your successes, no matter how small they may seem.

Why Celebrating Success is Important

When you are dealing with an addiction, it can be easy to focus only on your failures and setbacks. You may feel as though you are always falling short and that nothing you do is ever good enough.

This negative mindset can be a major barrier to recovery, as it can make you feel as though you are powerless to change.

Celebrating your successes, on the other hand, can help you to stay motivated and focused on your goals. When you acknowledge and celebrate the progress that you have made, no matter how small it may seem, you are reinforcing positive behaviours and building momentum for further progress.

How to Celebrate Successes

There are many different ways to celebrate your successes, and the method that works best for you will depend on your personality and preferences. However, here are a few suggestions to get you started:

1. Keep a journal: One of the simplest ways to celebrate your successes is to keep a journal of your progress. Write down your accomplishments, no matter how small they may seem, and take the time to reflect on the positive changes that you have made.

2. Treat yourself: When you reach a milestone in your recovery, take the time to treat yourself to something that you enjoy. This could be anything from a

special meal to a day trip to a place that you have always wanted to visit.

3. Share your success: Don't be afraid to share your successes with others. Whether it's a friend, family member, or support group, sharing your progress with others can help to build a sense of community and support.

4. Set new goals: Once you have celebrated your success, it's important to set new goals for yourself. This will help you to stay motivated and focused on your recovery and give you something to strive for.

5. Celebrate the small things: Remember, success is not always measured by big milestones. Celebrate the small victories,

such as a day without gambling or a positive interaction with a loved one.

Tips for Staying Motivated

While celebrating your successes is important, it's also important to stay motivated in the long term. Here are a few tips to help you stay on track:

1. Build a support network: Surround yourself with people who will support you and encourage you in your recovery. This could include friends, family members, support groups, or a therapist.

2. Take it one day at a time: Recovery is a journey, and it's important to take things one day at a time. Focus on the progress that you have made and the small steps

that you can take each day to move forward.

3. Practice self-care: Taking care of yourself is essential for staying motivated and focused on your recovery. Make time for exercise, relaxation, and other activities that help you to feel good.

4. Find healthy outlets: Instead of turning to gambling when you feel stressed or anxious, find healthy outlets for your emotions. This could include exercise, art, or spending time in nature.

5. Stay accountable: Keep yourself accountable by tracking your progress and regularly checking in with your support network. This will help you to stay focused and motivated, even when things get tough.

Forgive yourself:

Forgive yourself for past mistakes and move forward with a positive attitude.

Gambling addiction is a serious problem that can have severe consequences, both for the gambler and those around them. The good news is that recovery is possible, and one of the essential steps in the recovery process is learning to forgive oneself for past mistakes and move forward with a positive attitude.

In this chapter, we will discuss some tips on how to forgive oneself for past mistakes and move forward with a positive attitude when stopping gambling.

1. Acknowledge Your Mistakes

The first step in forgiving yourself is to acknowledge your mistakes. It can be challenging to admit to yourself and others that you have a problem, but it is an essential step in the recovery process.

Acknowledging your mistakes allows you to take responsibility for your actions, and it shows that you are willing to change. It is crucial to recognize that making mistakes is a part of being human, and it is how we learn and grow.

2. Accept Your Feelings

It is normal to experience a range of emotions when trying to forgive yourself for past mistakes. You may feel shame, guilt, or regret.

It is essential to accept these feelings and not try to push them away. Acknowledging and accepting your feelings can help you move forward and start the healing process.

3. Practice Self-Compassion

Self-compassion is an essential aspect of forgiving oneself. It involves treating oneself with kindness, understanding, and patience. Self-compassion means recognizing that you are not perfect, and it is okay to make mistakes. It is also about being gentle with oneself when experiencing difficult emotions.

4. Learn from Your Mistakes

Learning from your mistakes is essential in moving forward. Reflect on what led you to gamble and how you can avoid these triggers in the future.

Make a plan for what you will do if you feel the urge to gamble again. It is crucial to learn from your mistakes to avoid making the same ones in the future.

5. Focus on the Present

Focusing on the present moment can help you move forward and not dwell on the past. Set small goals for yourself and celebrate your successes. Taking small steps can help you build momentum and give you a sense of accomplishment.

Focusing on the present also means being mindful of your thoughts and emotions and not getting caught up in negative self-talk.

6. Seek Support

Recovering from gambling addiction can be challenging, and seeking support can be helpful. There are many resources available, such as support groups and counselling.

Talking to others who have gone through a similar experience can be comforting and can help you feel less alone. Seeking support can also provide you with practical advice on how to move forward.

7. Practice Gratitude

Practicing gratitude can help you shift your focus from negative thoughts to positive ones. Make a list of things that you are grateful for, no matter how small they may seem. Focusing on the good things in your life can help you maintain a positive attitude and keep you motivated.

In conclusion, forgiving oneself for past mistakes and moving forward with a positive attitude when stopping gambling is a crucial aspect of recovery. It takes time, patience, and effort, but it is possible. Acknowledge your mistakes, accept your feelings, practice self-compassion, learn from your mistakes, focus on the present, seek support, and practice gratitude. By following these tips, you can forgive yourself and move forward with a positive attitude. Remember that recovery is a journey, and it is okay to make mistakes along the way. Keep moving forward and believe in yourself.

Stay focused on your goals:

Stay focused on your goals and remember why you decided to quit gambling.

Quitting gambling can be a challenging process, but it is undoubtedly worth the effort. If you have made the decision to stop gambling, you have taken a significant step towards a healthier and happier life.

However, staying focused on your goals and remembering why you decided to quit gambling can be difficult, especially in the face of temptations and triggers.

In this chapter, we will explore some strategies that can help you stay focused and committed to your goal of quitting gambling.

1. Set clear and realistic goals

The first step in staying focused on your goals is to set clear and realistic goals. What do you want to achieve by quitting gambling? Do you want to save money, improve your relationships, or reduce your stress levels? Whatever your goals may be, it is essential to write them down and make them specific, measurable, achievable, relevant, and time-bound (SMART). Having SMART goals will help you stay focused and motivated, as you will be able to track your progress and celebrate your achievements along the way.

2. Identify your triggers and avoid them

One of the biggest challenges in quitting gambling is dealing with triggers. Triggers are situations, people, or emotions that make you want to gamble. For example, seeing a casino advertisement or being in a social situation where gambling is present can be a trigger. To stay focused on your goals, you need to identify your triggers and avoid them as much as possible. If you cannot avoid a trigger, try to change your response to it. For example, if you feel tempted to gamble after seeing a casino advertisement, try to distract yourself by doing something else, such as going for a walk or calling a friend.

3. Build a support system

Having a support system is crucial when quitting gambling. You need people who will encourage you, listen to you, and hold you accountable. Your support system can include family members, friends, a therapist, a support group, or a mentor. It is essential to communicate your goals and progress with your support system regularly. They can help you stay focused and remind you why you decided to quit gambling in the first place.

4. Practice self-care

Self-care is an essential aspect of staying focused on your goals. When you take care of your physical, emotional, and mental health, you will be better equipped to deal with challenges and resist temptations. Some self-care strategies you can try include:

- Getting enough sleep: Aim for 7-9 hours of sleep per night.

- Eating a healthy diet: Choose foods that nourish your body and avoid junk food and sugary drinks.

- Exercising regularly: Find a physical activity you enjoy and do it consistently.

- Practicing relaxation techniques: Try meditation, yoga, deep breathing, or progressive muscle relaxation.

- Engaging in hobbies: Find activities that you enjoy and that do not involve gambling, such as reading, painting, or playing music.

5. Celebrate your progress

Finally, it is essential to celebrate your progress and achievements along the way. Quitting gambling is a challenging journey, and it can be easy to focus on the negative aspects. However, it is crucial to acknowledge and celebrate the positive changes you have made. This can include anything from saving money to improving your relationships to feeling less stressed. Celebrating your progress can help you stay motivated and remind you why you decided to quit gambling in the first place.

In conclusion, staying focused on your goals and remembering why you decided to quit gambling is crucial for a successful recovery. By setting clear and realistic goals, identifying your triggers, building a support system, practicing self-care, and celebrating your progress, you can stay motivated and committed to your goal of quitting gambling. Remember, recovery is a journey, not a destination, and it takes time and effort.

Never give up:

Never give up on your journey to quit gambling, even if you experience setbacks or relapses.

Quitting gambling can be a challenging journey, but it is not impossible. It takes time, effort, and commitment to overcome this addiction. One of the most critical factors in this journey is the ability to persevere through setbacks and relapses.

The following are some tips on how to never give up on your journey to quit gambling, even if you experience setbacks or relapses.

1. Acceptance

The first step in overcoming setbacks and relapses is to accept that they are a natural part of the recovery process. Addiction is a chronic disease that requires ongoing management, and setbacks are bound to happen. Accepting this reality can help you prepare for the challenges ahead and develop a more resilient mindset.

2. Recognize triggers

Identifying the triggers that lead you to gamble can help you avoid them or develop strategies to manage them. Common triggers include stress, boredom, loneliness, and financial problems. Once you recognize your triggers, you can develop healthy coping mechanisms that can replace gambling as a way to deal with difficult emotions.

3. Seek support

Having a support system can make a world of difference in your recovery journey. You can seek support from friends, family, support groups, or a therapist. Surrounding yourself with people who understand your struggles and can provide you with encouragement and guidance can help you stay motivated and focused on your goals.

4. Set realistic goals

Setting unrealistic goals can set you up for failure and disappointment. Instead, set small, achievable goals that can build momentum and lead to more significant successes. Celebrating each small victory can help you stay motivated and keep moving forward.

5. Practice self-care

Self-care is crucial for maintaining mental and emotional well-being. Engaging in activities that promote relaxation, such as meditation, exercise, or spending time in nature, can help you manage stress and reduce the urge to gamble.

6. Learn from setbacks

Setbacks and relapses can be discouraging, but they can also provide valuable lessons. Instead of dwelling on your failures, take the opportunity to learn from them. Ask yourself what triggered the relapse and what you could have done differently. Use this knowledge to develop better strategies for managing future challenges.

7. Stay positive

Maintaining a positive attitude can be challenging when you are facing setbacks, but it is essential to stay hopeful and optimistic. Surround yourself with positivity by reading motivational books, listening to uplifting music, or spending time with people who inspire you.

8. Celebrate progress

It is essential to celebrate progress, no matter how small. Recognizing your accomplishments can boost your confidence and motivate you to keep going. Celebrate milestones, such as completing a month without gambling or reaching a financial goal.

9. Be patient

Recovery is a process that takes time, and it is essential to be patient and kind to yourself. Do not expect to overcome your addiction overnight, and do not beat yourself up when you experience setbacks. Remember that each day is a new opportunity to make progress.

In conclusion, quitting gambling is a challenging but achievable goal. Setbacks and relapses are a natural part of the recovery process, but with determination, support, and perseverance, you can overcome them.

Remember to be patient, kind to yourself, and seek help when you need it. Celebrate your progress, no matter how small, and stay positive and hopeful about your future. With these tips, you can stay focused on your journey and never give up on your goal to quit gambling.

www.chrisallton.com

Printed in Great Britain
by Amazon